DESIGN AND ENGINEERING

HI-TECH FASHION

Richard Spilsbury

⊗ Raintree

Raintree is an imprint of Capstone Global Library Limited, a company incorporated in England and Wales having its registered office at 7 Pilgrim Street, London, EC4V 6LB – Registered company number: 6695582

To contact Raintree please phone 0845 6044371, fax + 44 (0)1865 312263, or email myorders@raintreepublishers.co.uk. Customers from outside the UK please telephone +44 1865 312262.

Text © Capstone Global Library Limited 2013
First published in hardback in 2013
Paperback edition first published in 2014
The moral rights of the proprietor have been asserted.

Edited by Andrew Farrow, Abby Colich, and
  Vaarunika Dharmapala
Designed by Richard Parker
Original illustrations © Capstone Global Library
  Ltd 2013
Illustrations by HL Studios
Picture research by Elizabeth Alexander
Originated by Capstone Global Library Ltd
Printed and bound in China by CTPS

ISBN 978 1 406 24976 7 (hardback)
16 15 14 13 12
10 9 8 7 6 5 4 3 2 1

ISBN 978 1 406 24981 1 (paperback)
17 16 15 14 13
10 9 8 7 6 5 4 3 2 1

Acknowledgements
We would like to thank the following for permission to reproduce photographs: Alamy pp. 14 (© London Entertainment), 15 (© ClassicStock), 31 (© Image Source), 34 (© NorthScape), 36 (© Lonely Planet Images), 37 (© Joerg Boethling), 40 (© Olivier Asselin); © BioCouture 2007 p. 49 (Gary Wallis); Corbis pp. 9 & 10 (© Frank Leonhardt/DPA), 35 (© Qilai Shen/In Pictures); Courtesy of CoolShirt Systems p. 45; Genee Kegel/www.fabricanltd.com p. 24; Getty Images pp. 7 (Matt Cardy), 16 (Chris McGrath), 19 (David Paul Morris/Bloomberg via Getty Images), 20 (Johannes Simon/AFP), 21 (Bryan Bedder/WireImage for Vogue), 27 (STR/AFP), 28 (Emmanuel Dunand/AFP), 33 left (Alex Grimm), 33 right (Khem Sovannara/AFP), 42 (Goh Seng Chong/Bloomberg via Getty Images), 46 (Fethi Belaid/AFP), 48 (Erika Santelices/AFP); Image courtesy of SATRA Technology Centre p. 18; Image Courtesy of The Advertising Archives p. 43; NASA p. 22; Science Photo Library pp. 8 (Philippe Psaila), 25 (Eye Of Science); Shutterstock pp. 4 (© TFoxFoto), 5 (© Eduard Kyslynskyy), 11 (© urfin), 44 main (© Tom Wang) 44 inset (© John Kasawa); design feature arrows Shutterstock (© MisterElements).

Cover photograph of Rihanna performing on the first night of her UK tour, 7 May, 2010 in Birmingham, England, reproduced with permission of Getty Images (Matt Kent/WireImage).

CONTENTS

Some words are shown in bold, **like this**. You can find out what they mean by looking in the glossary.

FASHIONABLE WORLD

Most of us care about the clothes we wear. They go beyond providing protection from the elements or from dangers we may face in our work. They are a way of displaying identity. People in the army or fire service wear uniforms partly to help them feel like members of a team. When we wear clothes of a style we like, it can have a positive effect on how we feel about ourselves. Taste in clothes can even affect how we relate to others.

Global industry

In some countries, such as Italy and Hong Kong, fashion is an important part of the local economy. In fact, fashion is a major global industry, too. It provides a variety of jobs for millions of people. For example, farmers grow crops such as cotton from which clothes are made, textile mill workers transform raw materials into fabrics, fashion designers come up with ideas for the garments we wear, and shop assistants help to sell them.

Firefighters risk being burnt and breathing in smoke or fumes when working. Wearing the right protective clothing is critical to their survival and ability to do the job.

Technology

All fashion is partly the product of technology. Technology is the process of using technical knowledge to modify natural materials for meeting human needs and wants. Just as trees are transformed through technology into paper and building materials, so anything from oil to wool is used to make the textiles we wear. Fashion is also partly the product of economics. Companies will only invest time and money in researching materials, employing designers, setting up factories, and opening shops if they are confident it will make them money.

What is hi-tech fashion?

Hi-tech is a term that means using new, innovative, or complicated technology. It is applied to all sorts of products ranging from computer processors to fashion. Hi-tech fashion is clothing that incorporates up-to-date technical features to give particular properties. These include keeping the wearer warm by reducing heat loss or stopping them from getting wet.

Trousers suitable for snowboarding are usually made from waterproof materials to keep the boarder dry. Hi-tech features may also include seams and shaping at the knee to help the trousers bend easily, and zips at the thighs to control leg temperature.

Important terms

Throughout this book you will come across some important terms relating to fashion or clothing, that also apply to most other products. It will be helpful to explain some of these before you meet them so you can get the most out of the information in the book.

Product life cycle

A fly hatches from an egg, grows, and eventually dies. That is its life cycle. Products also have life cycles that begin with ideas and design. They continue with acquiring materials to make the product through to making, using, and also disposing of the product after use.

Sustainability

A product's life cycle can have different environmental impacts. For example, drilling for the oil used to make some fabrics can cause pollution. **Sustainability** is when a process can be maintained at a steady level for long periods without causing environmental or social damage. In the fashion industry, waste, energy, and water use may be reduced to make processes more sustainable.

Requirements

When companies decide to make a product for sale they have a list of design **requirements**. There are two sorts of requirements:

- **Criteria**: goals that must be satisfied to make a product that sells. So, a boat's criteria would be that it floats, moves fast through the water, and looks attractive.
- **Constraints**: requirements that limit how the product is made. Major constraints are cost and safety. For example, to make a boat cheap enough to sell to lots of people, it might have to be made of cheaper, heavier, less attractive materials than a boat that would cost more.

Balancing the criteria and constraints to make a product that will attract consumers and not break the bank for manufacturers is sometimes called a trade-off.

Engineering design

You might think of engineering as building bridges or skyscrapers, but in more general terms it is the process of turning ideas into working products, such as a television or a waterproof coat. Design is central to the engineering process but there is rarely a single, right design solution to a problem. One is chosen from several options that are evaluated, tested, and adjusted to improve them. The process involves:

defining the problem

gathering information

generating multiple solutions

analysing and selecting solutions

testing and finalizing solutions

Any piece of fashion is the result of an **engineering design** process. The pattern, colour, shape, and materials were chosen and optimized to meet design requirements.

Optimization

This is the process of improving design to achieve the best possible product. For example, you make a paper aeroplane, try it out, and then refold or redesign it to make it fly further. Two parts of the **optimization** process are:

- **Modelling**: when design solutions are visualized to see what they might be like. This is usually done by making 2-D or 3-D computer images or videos.
- **Prototypes**: full-scale working models of chosen designs using actual materials that are constructed to see what the finished products will be like.

FASHION MEETS TECHNOLOGY

Hi-tech clothing is a growing area of fashion. More and more garments have hi-tech features that enhance their effectiveness or attract a broader range of buyers. So, what sorts of hi-tech clothing items are there?

Functional hi-tech

Different types of garments use different technologies to achieve their design criteria and meet specific functions. The following are some common types:

- *Keeping warm*: down jackets, synthetic foam, wool, and fleece all insulate or trap air warmed by the body next to the skin and prevent it from escaping. Some other hi-tech clothing has built-in wires that heat up when electricity passes through them, keeping the wearer warm.
- *Staying cool and dry*: some fabrics channel sweat away from skin to create a cooling effect. Other garments have built-in electric fans!
- *Reducing odour*: some garments, such as underwear or shoes, have built in chemicals that prevent the build-up of bacteria on sweat. These organisms are responsible for making the substances that cause smelly body odour.
- *Increasing fitness*: some types of shoes such as Fitflops and MBT (Maasai Barefoot Technology) have specially shaped soles to increase muscle activity in the back and legs and reduce stress to joints while walking.

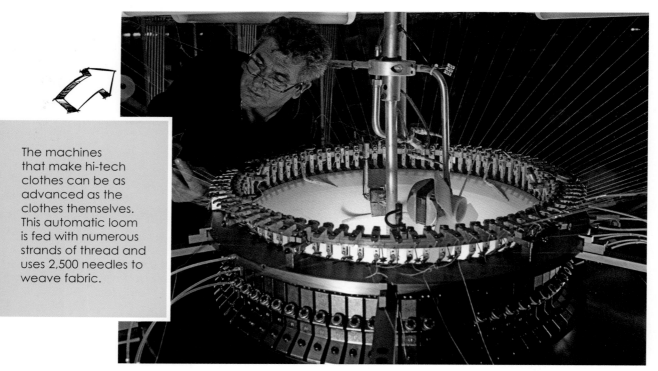

The machines that make hi-tech clothes can be as advanced as the clothes themselves. This automatic loom is fed with numerous strands of thread and uses 2,500 needles to weave fabric.

Feelgood hi-tech

Some hi-tech fashion is all about making the wearer feel happier. Technology that can make the wearer stand out from the crowd includes invisible, light-sensitive tattoos that show up in places with UV lights, such as nightclubs. Robotic dresses are very eye-catching – they have inbuilt motors that at the flick of a button can change length or shape! Some garments even have an emotional impact. For example, the Hug Dress has built in sensors that detect the wearer hugging themselves. It can link via Bluetooth to a mobile to send the hug to another person wearing another Hug Dress.

This jacket has an integrated solar panel. It provides a portable power supply for electronic gadgets such as mobile phones.

CONTRAST THE PAST

The first bullet-proof vests were probably the waistcoats lined with steel plates worn by Union officers in the American Civil War (1861–1865). They were rigid, heavy, and ineffective against rifle bullets. Today's bullet-proof vests are mostly made of a woven material called Kevlar. They are light, flexible, and stop more powerful bullets than in the past.

Kevlar vests are bulky, however, and are typically worn by soldiers and police. Fashion designers such as Miguel Caballero make light, thin bullet-proof garments that look like normal clothing. They are often worn by important politicians at public events where they could get shot.

Hi-tech demand

A major reason for hi-tech demand is changes to technology. Since the 1980s, there has been a global increase in reliance on electronic devices, from digital timers on machines to mobile phones. This is because of widening networks of communication, and efficient marketing that has persuaded people gadgets are essential for life in the modern world.

As many people today carry around gadgets, it is not surprising that new features such as built-in microphones and holes for headphone wires are increasingly common in the clothes we buy.

Why hi-tech?

Using hi-tech materials or features benefits manufacturers in different ways. Consumers may accept they need to pay more for hi-tech fashion because it is the product of scientific research or because it is the best available. For example, people with a functional need for a warm jacket might pay more for a thermal jacket tested by Antarctic explorers because the technology has been proven in the most demanding conditions. Using hi-tech breathable or durable materials on fashion garments can make them appear less frivolous and encourage consumers to pay high prices. This is one reason why fashion houses such as Prada and Zegna used them in their 2010 collections.

Variable life cycle

Demand for any fashion, not just hi-tech, can change quickly because **fashion trends** – ideas about what "looks good" – change. This is one reason why some garments are not used for long. Millions of perfectly good clothing items are thrown into landfill sites each year. Length of use also depends on the quality of materials the garment is made from and the price paid – people may feel happier to discard something that was cheap. Length of use is just one aspect affecting a garment's life cycle. Some materials are not as durable as others or may contain materials that are difficult to **recycle**.

Average spending per person on clothing (2007)

population 301 million
spend per person $1,429

People who buy lots of clothes each year tend to throw away more of them, too. Some of the shortest garment life cycles tend to be in richer countries where, generally, people have more to spend on fashion.

population 1,321 million
spend per person $73

population 61 million
spend per person $1,438

population 1,130 million
spend per person $25

UK	US	China	India
UK	**US**	**China**	**India**
US$88 billion	US$430 billion	US$96 billion	US$28 billion

LIFE CYCLE OF A HI-TECH GARMENT

The life history of a hi-tech garment, such as a waterproof coat, may be long or short. This depends on how long it took to design, create materials for, manufacture, transport to shops, and how long the garment was worn for. It also depends on whether it had further users or whether its materials were recycled. The diagram on these pages summarizes the main stages of the coat's life history, which are broadly the same for any item of clothing.

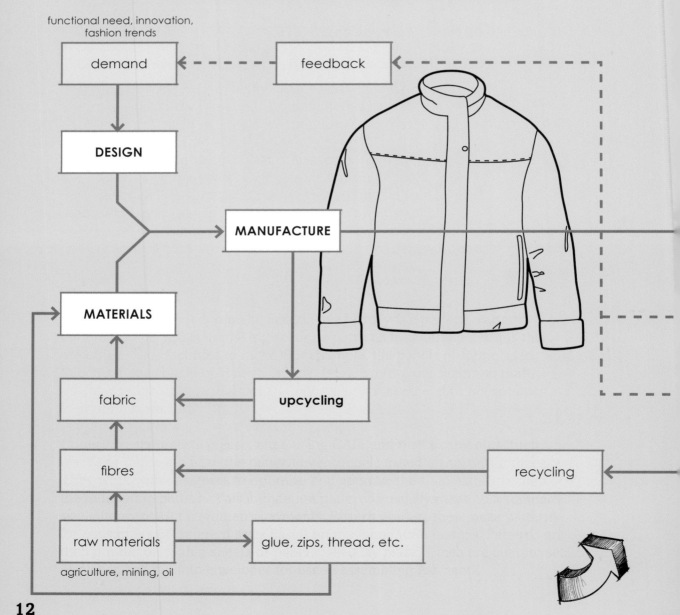

functional need, innovation, fashion trends

demand ← feedback

DESIGN

MANUFACTURE

MATERIALS

fabric ← upcycling

fibres ← recycling

raw materials → glue, zips, thread, etc.

agriculture, mining, oil

Ins and outs

Each stage of the life cycle has many inputs. All stages require human input in terms of employees' work and time, from factory workers to salespeople. Most stages require electricity or other energy sources to power machines as well as resources such as water. Some stages require materials. For example, making a zip may require metal, a raw material which is usually mined from under the ground. Many stages also have outputs, such as waste materials and products. The lifetime use of energy and resources is impacted by recycling. If recycled fibres are used to make the jacket, then this uses fewer resources than making new fibres from raw materials.

The dashed arrows in the diagram show **feedback** from shops and customers. Clothing companies survive by selling garments. Therefore, they need to know what people want to buy before coming up with ideas for new designs and investing in new garments.

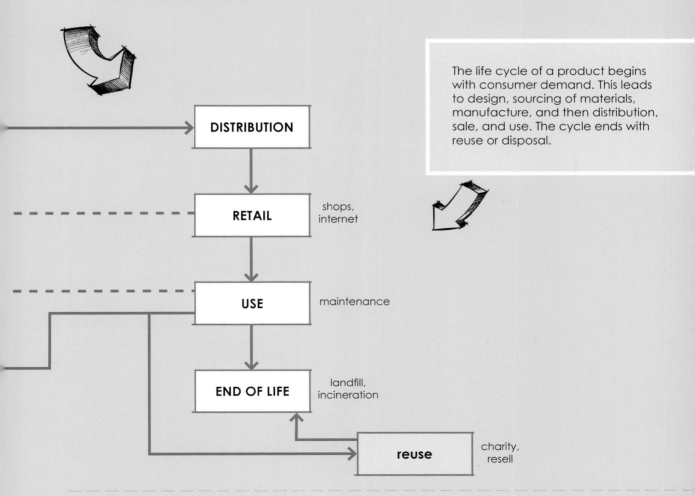

The life cycle of a product begins with consumer demand. This leads to design, sourcing of materials, manufacture, and then distribution, sale, and use. The cycle ends with reuse or disposal.

DISTRIBUTION

RETAIL shops, internet

USE maintenance

END OF LIFE landfill, incineration

reuse charity, resell

FASHION DESIGN

The first stage in creating a hi-tech garment is to come up with a design. How do designers come up with ideas?

Fashion inspirations and needs

Clothing design is driven in two main ways. The first is to meet people's desire to be fashionable. Designers have many inspirations, such as what high-profile media personalities wear. For example, the geeky clothes used in the television series *Glee* in 2010 and 2011 influenced the styles of clothes bought by teenagers.

The clothes and costumes worn by pop stars such as Lady Gaga could end up in the shops in a modified form for anyone to buy.

The other driver of hi-tech fashion design is meeting general and specific needs. The NFL American football league assesses hundreds of players who hope to be signed up to teams. There were concerns that the tests were not always fair – different coaches and experts might assess players slightly differently. The company Under Armour designed a special vest with inbuilt sensors that not only measure a player's fitness, but also power, acceleration, and ability to change direction while running. This has made testing fairer because the same measurements are made for each player.

CONTRAST THE PAST

At the start of the 20th century, sportswear meant clothing men could wear when being active. At that time, women were normally not expected to be active other than taking gentle strolls or rides. Many wore clothing such as tight corsets to create a narrower waist and long, full skirts most of the time. The few sportswomen wore long, baggy ankle- or knee-length trousers called bloomers to cover their legs.

In the early 1920s, the French fashion designer "Coco" Chanel started a revolution in the way women dressed by making shorter garments made in a thin, slightly stretchy material called **jersey**. This was more commonly used to make men's underwear. Her sportswear designs were worn without corsets and allowed women to move more freely when active. Today, women's normal clothes in many parts of the world are made of light, loose fabrics such as jersey. Many women exercise and take part in sports or other activities wearing hi-tech sportswear such as stretchy **lycra** garments.

When winter sports became a popular leisure pursuit in the 1930s, people wore similar clothes to those they wore at home, such as woollen jumpers. Contrast this with the lycra suits and hi-tech plastic, insulated boots of today (see the picture on page 5).

Market changes

What is in fashion one month might not be the next. Therefore, clothing companies need to maximize their speed to market – that is, how fast they get products into shops. It is often more expensive for companies to make and ship garments faster, so they need to find the right balance of speed and cost in order to sell their garments at prices customers can afford.

Speed to market in fashion is typically several months, so fashion designers need to predict what might be popular in the future. Designers for high street shops often look at the one-off creations made for top fashion houses. They may create "copies" that mirror successful shapes, colours, patterns, or fabrics. They also use **market researchers** to analyse sales figures for different garments in shops, in different areas, and in different age groups. They find out what styles and materials sold well to help them predict future sales. Many large companies use trend forecasting services as well.

Elite athletes are big users of hi-tech clothing. Those who play in contact sports such as rugby and American football often wear protective body armour.

Case study: Lena Berglin

What do you think of mittens that connect to a mobile phone? You can talk into them when it is cold rather than taking them off to reach for a handset. Or a vest with tiny motors embedded in the fabric which press on soldiers' skin to alert them about warnings sent by radar signals? These are just some of the ideas of Lena Berglin, a Swedish designer of hi-tech garments. She does not build separate wires into the fabric, but rather adapts the threads used to make the garment so they can conduct electricity safely. Berglin says:

"You don't need a lot of extra equipment. You're wearing the garment, and fabrics are good to work with. They are functional."

First ideas

Fashion designers translate their first rough idea for a piece of clothing into several possible design solutions. They usually create lists of criteria and constraints for the garment, such as safety. For example, if there are going to be lights in a waterproof garment, the electric wiring needs to be safe in the wet. They consider **ergonomics** during design. This is the science of understanding and improving the interaction of people with products, equipment, or environments. For instance, a sports shirt needs most ventilation and moisture-reducing features under the arms and on the back, where people sweat the most.

Thinking of all the possible requirements is rarely left to one person. Designers may work in teams, for example with salespeople who know what shapes or features may sell best, to give feedback on the ideas. This process is often called **brainstorming**.

waterproof/breathable fabric

Tough/padded shoulders/elbows to withstand falls at speed

decorative strips that are luminous in the dark

clips on waist/arms to pull in and stop flapping in the wind

short enough to not ride up when sitting on bike

After a brainstorming session, designers will make rough sketches of their concept designs.

Taking form

Once designers have their concept designs, they start modelling. Designers use a variety of **digital tools**, such as graphics tablets and Computer-Aided Design (CAD) software, to create detailed visualizations of their ideas:

- two-dimensional (2-D) technical drawings to show the dimensions and shapes
- three-dimensional (3-D) illustrations to give a more accurate idea of the form
- animated videos to show how the garment will look, move, or operate from different angles

Modelling can help designers and other people in clothing companies to optimize their final designs. But clothing has to work on a real person and not just on a computer. This is why designers usually create a prototype. These are working models. Designers choose materials, for example nylon in the case of a waterproof (see pages 22–29 for more about materials). They cut, stitch, or glue the materials to make a garment that is worn and tested by models for fit. Many companies will take prototypes from individual designers and amend them further, to produce a first sample garment.

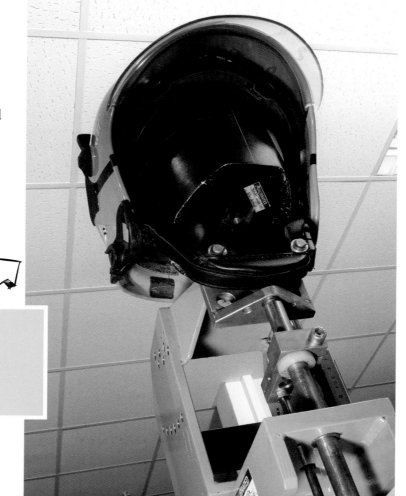

Here a special machine is testing the chinstrap strength or a firefighter's helmet.

Testing and choice

Garments undergo a variety of other tests depending on their features. For example, material strength, resistance to wear or cutting, how well it washes, whether the fastenings work repeatedly, wind or water resistance, warmth in cold conditions, and flammability may all be tested. Often, testing takes place in specialist independent laboratories. Once garments are fully tested and optimized, companies then make up garment samples of the final design choices.

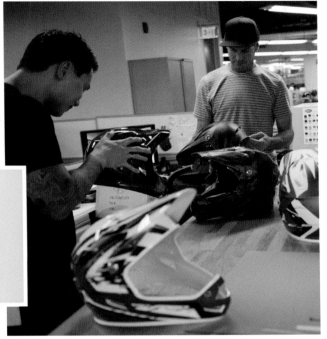

These members of a design team are examining several concept ideas for the outer shells of new bike helmets. The next stage in the engineering process is to make up prototypes for testing.

BRANDING

Branding refers to the ways companies highlight what makes their products different and better than their competitors'. It includes logos or designs that represent the company, such as the Nike swoosh, and associations with lifestyles, such as mountaineering or taking part in marathons. An important part of designing hi-tech fashion is to make it fit into a brand.

For example, a Timberland jacket may have large, rugged zips and patches on elbows to resist wear that would suit an outdoor lifestyle, even though it might be worn mostly in cities. Making garments fit an existing brand is specialized work, and many clothing companies get the help of branding or **public relations** companies to do this successfully.

Trade fairs

Many designers and companies produce small batches of garments to show at trade fairs or fashion weeks. They hope to sell their ideas to customers, such as retail outlets, before having the cost of manufacturing thousands. One of the biggest clothing trade shows is MAGIC, held in Las Vegas, USA, which is attended by thousands of fashion buyers.

At a trade fair, buyers can often see complete ranges of fashion items. They can examine the designs and material, then choose which ones they will purchase for sale to customers.

Design issues

Clothing designers, like other designers, often **patent** their work. This means registering the design with a government department to prove it is their creative property. Anyone wanting to use exactly the same idea may have to pay for permission to do so. Patents may cover anything from the overall design to new uses of hi-tech technology, and patterns of fabric used.

Counterfeiting

Counterfeiting of designs is a big problem in the industry. This is partly because patents may only apply to one country, and partly because there are so many garments produced that patent infringements are not noticed. In 2008 alone, over 100 million counterfeit garments were detected being smuggled into Europe, mostly made in China. To copy designs, companies may **reverse engineer** a garment. Counterfeiting and patent infringement can damage the reputation of a brand by being associated with poor-quality goods or poorly functioning copies of hi-tech materials.

Case study: CuteCircuit

CuteCircuit is a fashion company specializing in wearable technology. The founders of the company are Francesca Rosella, a fashion designer with an interest in technology, and Ryan Genz, a user interface designer. This means he works out how hi-tech features can be operated simply and efficiently by a garment's wearer.

Their designs, such as colour-changing dresses, have been **endorsed** by the pop star Katy Perry (right) and used in museum displays worldwide to demonstrate hi-tech fashion.

"We wouldn't make [our clothes] look so pretty and seamless and beautiful if we didn't spend a huge amount of time designing the circuits to make sure they did the right thing, that they didn't get too warm, and they could also be washed. So, the more you design it, the more you alter it, the better it gets."

This CuteCircuit dress is made of silky chiffon with over 3,000 tiny LED lights embedded within it. At the flick of a switch, the wearer can make LEDs of different colours shine so they make the dress appear to change colour.

WHAT HAVE WE LEARNED?

- Fashion design is the result of inspiration, research, and meeting the needs of consumers.
- Designers balance criteria and constraints to come up with ideas.
- Registering patents is important for designers to avoid theft of their ideas.

HI-TECH MATERIALS

Clothing design is closely linked with materials, and garments may use many different materials with varying properties. Designers are constantly working with scientists to create new, improved materials that fulfil their function better or differently from others.

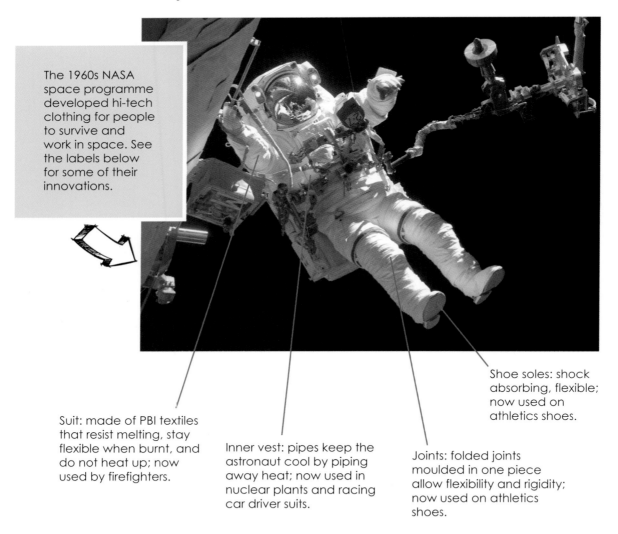

The 1960s NASA space programme developed hi-tech clothing for people to survive and work in space. See the labels below for some of their innovations.

Suit: made of PBI textiles that resist melting, stay flexible when burnt, and do not heat up; now used by firefighters.

Inner vest: pipes keep the astronaut cool by piping away heat; now used in nuclear plants and racing car driver suits.

Joints: folded joints moulded in one piece allow flexibility and rigidity; now used on athletics shoes.

Shoe soles: shock absorbing, flexible; now used on athletics shoes.

Material properties

Most clothing materials are made from either natural or **synthetic fibres**. **Natural fibres** come from living things such as cotton from cotton plants. Synthetic fibres are made in factories from minerals, such as **crude oil**, and from plant materials, such as wood pulp.

Materials can be given other properties by blending fibres. For example, blending thin lycra **microfibres** with polyester or cotton fibres makes stretchy fabrics that keep their shape. Adding polyester to cotton makes it dry quicker and need less ironing.

Choosing criteria

Properties of materials often overlap and designers choose which to use based on many criteria. For example, merino wool is warm, water resistant, and easily washable like polyester fleece. Both are ideal for warm garments. Although polyester fleece is much cheaper to produce, merino has other beneficial properties as well, such as being more breathable and resistant to body odour.

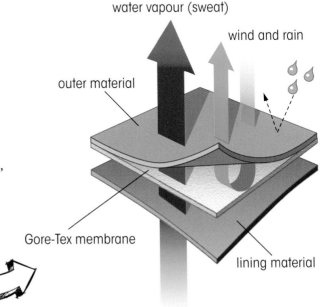

water vapour (sweat)

wind and rain

outer material

Gore-Tex membrane

lining material

Gore-Tex fabric is a good choice if the criteria required is keeping the wearer dry. It has two layers of fabric, with a membrane in between. The membrane keeps rain out while releasing sweat.

Here, you can compare the material properties of several different fabrics.

	source	absorbency	drying	breathability	warm/cool
natural					
cotton	cotton plant	high	slow	good	cool
linen	flax plant	high	fast	good	cool
wool	sheep	high	slow	good	warm
synthetic					
polyester	oil	low	fast	poor	cool
nylon	oil	high	slow	quite good	warm
acrylic	oil	low	fast	poor	warm

New materials

Material or textile engineers are people who not only test, assess, and improve existing materials, but also help make new ones. They work in laboratories, using maths and science to assess the properties of anything from natural fibres to metals, to create new hi-tech fabrics. They may find further uses for the materials they invent that could increase demand. For example, spray-on clothing was invented to make instant, close-fitting garments, but the technology has been adapted to create spray-on dressings for wounds.

Spray-on clothing is made using a liquid that becomes a fabric when sprayed on to a surface. Cotton and elastic synthetic fibres in the liquid link together as they dry. Spraying more layers makes thicker fabric. The fabric can be peeled off, washed, and worn again.

Tiny technology

Nanotechnology is engineering at a tiny scale. It is the complex science of adapting molecules to give them particular properties. Examples of nanotechnology that might be possible in the future include creating microscopic computer processors or mini robots that can detect and attack cancer cells. Nanotechnology is already being used to create hi-tech fibres and materials for clothing. For example, silver can kill many bacteria. Putting a coat of tiny silver particles on or within fibres can make fabric anti-bacterial.

INSPIRATION

Engineers get their inspiration for new materials from many different sources, including nature:

- *Burrs:* In 1948, a Swiss engineer saw how spiky burrs from plants stuck to animal fur. Tiny hooks on the burrs fastened on to loops of hair. He realized that a similar fastening system – a zipperless zipper called velcro – could be used for opening and closing garments quickly. Velcro gained popularity on NASA space missions and for ski suits, and is widely used today.

- *Sharks:* the company Speedo wanted to make swimsuits that could help athletes swim faster. Material engineers at Speedo worked with scientists at London's Natural History Museum to find out how big sharks can swim fast with little effort. They found that the pattern of tiny "teeth" on a shark's skin helps water to flow smoothly over it and reduce **drag**.

Engineers mimicked the shark skin texture for their Fastskin swimsuits, and swimmers set many world records wearing them. Engineers worked out that one tenth of the drag on a swimmer results from how water moves over their skin. The surface texture of the Fastskin suit reduced this drag considerably. For top swimmers, this was like giving them a 6-metre (20-feet) headstart in a 200-metre (656-foot) race.

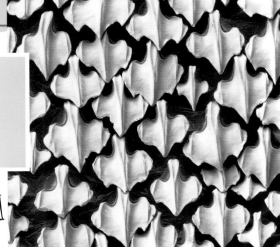

This is a close-up of shark's skin, showing the tooth-like scales. These act to reduce the drag on the shark as it swims.

Material impacts

Growing and processing raw materials into fibres and fabrics for clothing have an impact on the environment. For example, making synthetic fibres requires crude oil, which can spill on to land or sea during production and transport, harming wildlife and polluting freshwater. Processing nylon from oil releases nitrous oxide, which is harmful to people's breathing and is a **greenhouse gas** over 300 times better at storing heat than carbon dioxide. Greenhouse gases contribute to global warming.

Natural fibre production

Producing natural fibres can also cause environmental problems. For example, growing the global cotton crop uses around 15 per cent of all pesticides used on Earth, which can pollute water and cause health problems for farmers. Less than 1 per cent of all cotton is grown organically, which means using no poisonous chemicals that cause long-term damage to the environment. Organic cotton is more expensive because it requires more labour to tend to the cotton plants. Some other conventional fibre crops, such as bamboo and hemp, typically use fewer pesticides, less fertilizer, and less water per kilogram of fibre grown, than cotton. However, people often use harmful chemicals to soften their tough fibres for making smooth fabrics.

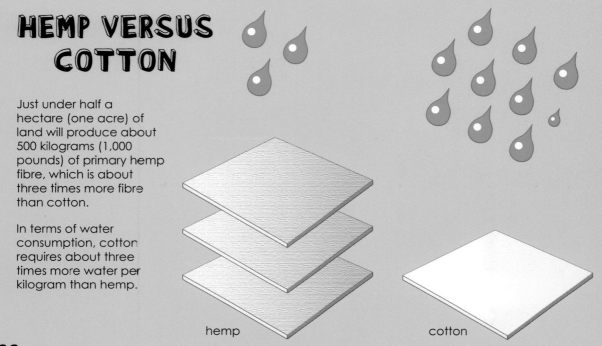

HEMP VERSUS COTTON

Just under half a hectare (one acre) of land will produce about 500 kilograms (1,000 pounds) of primary hemp fibre, which is about three times more fibre than cotton.

In terms of water consumption, cotton requires about three times more water per kilogram than hemp.

hemp   cotton

Recycled fibres

Creating recycled fibres has a lower environmental impact than farming or drilling for more of the raw materials. For example, polyurethane drinks bottles may be shredded and transformed into fibres for use in hi-tech fleeces, such as Polartec. Used rubber, such as old tyres, can be made into the soles of Ecotrax climbing shoes. Using recycled plastic like this cuts down use of oil. Similarly, recycled cotton or wool, made by using waste from factories or by taking apart old garments, has a lower impact than farming new fibres.

Making textiles from any fibre can involve dyeing. Waste dye is often discharged into rivers, and the chemicals it contains, such as dioxins, get into drinking water. When dioxins are consumed by people, they can affect normal hormone production or cause cancers.

Choosing materials

Fashion designers and companies creating hi-tech clothing have access to an enormous range of materials. They may use the services of specialist materials advisors to help them choose which to use. For example, Materials Connexion is a global organization that keeps an up-to-date collection of materials for many industries, not only fashion. It advises companies on the best materials for different purposes and also on future trends in materials. In 2011, for instance, the material neoprene was widely tipped to be a key material for fashion in 2012.

The final choice of materials is based on balancing cost and performance with a range of other engineering design criteria and constraints. For example, some designers and companies may choose sustainably produced materials for their hi-tech clothes. The distance materials need to be transported from where they are produced to factories or consumers is a major issue. Transport vehicles use up fuel and release greenhouse gases. Sustainable materials are often more expensive because they are less common. However, they may be chosen by designers because they will attract consumers keen to lower their environmental impact when buying clothes.

This animal rights activist is carrying out a protest against shops that sell products made of fur.

Ethical choices

Ethics is another constraint for some consumers. For example, vegans eat no animal products and often avoid leather. To attract a vegan audience for their clothing, designers need to use synthetic leather alternatives or equivalently performing natural fibres, such as hemp.

ECO IMPACT

The clothing company Rapanui is unusual in that it traces where the materials in its clothes are grown or sourced, how it is processed and transported, and the journey from seed to shop. It uses wind power in some of its factories and prefers slower shipping transport to air freight because it has a lower environmental impact. By being open about where its clothes are from, Rapanui allows customers to make an informed choice about whether they want to buy its products.

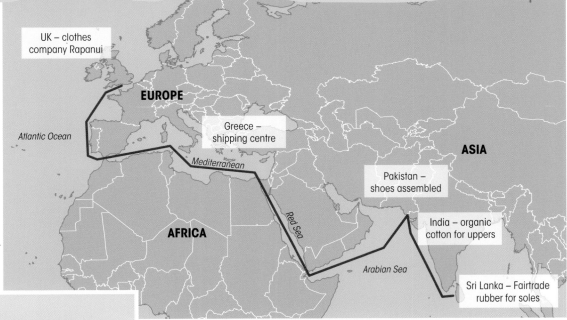

This traceability map is for a pair of casual shoes made by Rapanui. Rubber for the soles is from responsibly managed plantations in Sri Lanka, and cotton for the uppers from India. These materials are made up into shoes in Pakistan and transported by ship to the United Kingdom.

WHAT HAVE WE LEARNED?

- Materials have different properties.
- New materials are constantly being created.
- Choosing materials is based on cost, function, and sustainability.

MANUFACTURING HI-TECH FASHION

The manufacture of hi-tech fashion involves translating a one-off design into many identical garment copies. Factories are systems that require inputs, including not only materials and designs, but also workers and energy. The prime output is products for sale.

Material input

Materials come into factories from many specialist manufacturers. They may be generic parts, such as zips, or specific parts for particular garments, such as inflatable pumps for shoes or insulating coats. Materials include:

- rolls of textiles from cotton, wool, and other textile mills
- pieces of leather or suede from tanneries
- chemicals such as dyes, waterproofing compounds, and plastic granules to be formed into soles
- fasteners such as zips, Velcro, and studs
- assembling materials ranging from sewing thread to glues
- decorative materials such as logos, tags, piping, and sequins
- finishing materials such as stones to stone-wash denim.

The pattern

The first thing needed to make fashion in a factory is a pattern. Pattern cutters are specialists in making accurate patterns for clothing designs that are efficient for factories to make. For example, the panels of fabric used to construct a coat should have enough fabric around the seams so that machines cannot leave gaps when they are sewn together, but not so much that fabric is wasted.

Cutters create pattern pieces, often using CAD, and may **drape** and stitch pieces of fabric cut from the pattern over models called forms or dummies. They work with designers to optimize and approve the final pattern, called the foundation pattern. This foundation pattern is usually made to a standard size, often size 10 for women's garments. Pattern graders then make patterns for consumers of different sizes based on the foundation pattern. Patterns are then printed on to thin sheets of paper, called lay plans, which are cut into sets of pieces and put into envelopes for use in assembling garments.

The lay plans allow the manufacturer to work out the quantity and cost of materials needed. If the process is done using CAD, the lay plans are printed and checked digitally.

Some fashion factories store hundreds of textile rolls. They may use them to make prototype garments, and in the process set up the cutting and sewing machines ready to make large numbers of designs.

ECO IMPACT

People working in shoe factories may have to use strong glues to stick shoe soles or other **components** to the leather or fabric uppers. Many commonly used glues are types of plastics, such as styrene, dissolved in organic **solvents** such as benzene. Once the glue is spread, the solvent evaporates leaving the plastic sticking the sole on.

The chemicals in evaporating solvents, or **VOCs**, pollute the atmosphere and can also be very harmful to factory workers unless proper health and safety procedures are in place. They can cause anything from short-term dizziness, headaches, or nausea, through to nerve and psychological disorders, and damage to major organs such as kidneys and the liver.

Production

There are three major manufacturing processes that take place during garment production. What is required at each stage depends on the design, the complexity of the pattern, and the materials used.

- *Cutting*: fabric is spread out and the pattern pieces are arranged, glued, or stapled on to the fabric. The marked fabric is then cut into pieces using a variety of machines. These range from circular cutting blades that move around pattern edges and sharp stamping machines that chop out whole pieces, to lasers that accurately melt or burn through fabric.
- *Sewing*: the fabric pieces are stitched together using powerful machines capable of creating over 8,000 stitches per minute. Different sewing machines are used for different parts of a garment. For example, some are just for button holes, and others are used to sew paddings or linings.
- *Finishing*: includes washing, adding buttons, tags, and other details, and pressing. Pressing involves steam ironing to remove creases, to add pleats and folds, and to accentuate shapes.

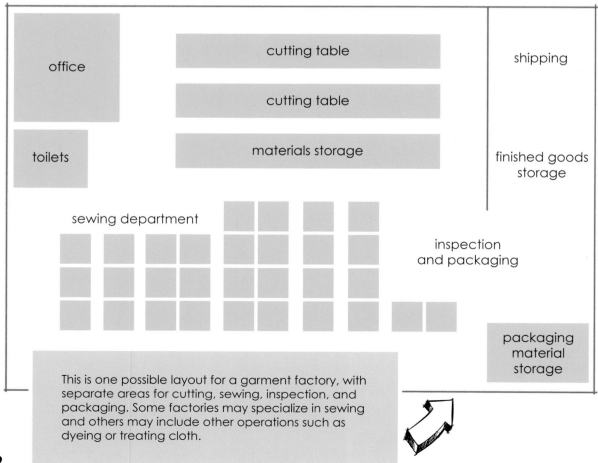

This is one possible layout for a garment factory, with separate areas for cutting, sewing, inspection, and packaging. Some factories may specialize in sewing and others may include other operations such as dyeing or treating cloth.

Work flow

Factory managers coordinate work flow through a factory. They calculate how many operations of production – such as sewing sleeves or gluing on soles – a garment needs to meet its **specifications**. They also work out how long each operation will take. In some factories, garments move to the next operation straight after finishing the previous one. In others, a batch of garments moves together from operation to operation. The machines and specialist operators, such as cutting or sewing machinists, are arranged through the factory in a production line. Garments may move from one unit to the next on **conveyor belts** or through chutes to speed up the production process.

Above: a worker is piercing shoelace holes in a football boot.
Right: these workers are checking the quality of sewn garments.

CONTRAST THE PAST

Until the late 19th century, clothes and shoes were usually made by hand. Tailors and cobblers measured people for **bespoke** items. By the mid-20th century, nearly all clothing was made to standard sizes in factories as ready-to-wear clothing. Bespoke tailoring is now rare because it is expensive, highly skilled work.

However, today it is possible to have relatively cheap bespoke garments made. People can stand in 3-D **body scanners** that accurately measure their posture and body dimensions to within a fraction of a millimetre. The data is then sent to automated cutting and sewing machines in factories.

Fashion factories

Companies may use factories of their own to make up their hi-tech clothing. Sometimes they set up new factories from scratch. There are different reasons for this. For example, the British outdoor clothing manufacturer Páramo set up a new factory to make its waterproof and fleece jackets in Bogota, Colombia, because its owner wanted to create employment for disadvantaged women there. Sometimes companies make garments at their own existing factories or adapt them for hi-tech manufacture by installing electronics in fabrics, computer cutting, or special bonding of materials.

Many companies send designs electronically to the factory, to be used in Computer-Aided Manufacture (CAM). This can include matching colours to the design and the automatic printing of fabrics, as well as controlling the cutting and joining of pieces.

In the 19th century, Lancashire towns such as Manchester were the largest cotton textile producers in the world. They were centres of innovation for cotton processing, and also had access to rivers and coal. This meant they could easily power spinning and weaving machines.

Constraints on factories

Constraints on clothing factories include the availability of water for washing or other finishing processes, electricity to operate factory machinery, and transport to distribute the finished garments. In most countries, constraints also include meeting legal requirements, such as dealing with waste and controlling pollution. This includes gases emitted into the atmosphere and dirty water entering rivers and seas.

Outsourcing

The major constraint on where a garment is made is cost. Buying land, setting up and running factories, and employing skilled workers is expensive, especially in more developed countries. It is usually cheaper for a European or US company to set up or use existing factories in less developed countries. This process is called **outsourcing** and is used by many large **globalized** clothing manufacturers, including Gap and Tesco.

There are many challenges associated with outsourcing, including difficulty controlling quality, longer manufacture and transport times, and criticism from consumers about unfavourable working conditions.

This Chinese factory is owned by the Baoxiniao Group. Baoxiniao makes about 1 million suits per year. Around 10 per cent of this is made for overseas companies such as Marks & Spencer.

CONTRAST THE PAST

Around 1900, New York City was the garment capital of the world. This success was due to the availability of cheap, skilled immigrant labour and US textiles. Today, around half of all global textiles and garments are made in China, especially near the coastal export centres in the south-east of the country. China's success is a result of accessible government loans for setting up modern export factories and the availability of materials such as Chinese-grown cotton fibres. The labour force making the garments is largely made up of **migrant workers**, many from rural villages across the country.

Factory conditions

Around 60 million people work in the textile, clothing, and footwear industries. Most are young women in less developed countries. The International Labour Organization, an agency of the United Nations, has a set of principles promoting decent work for all workers. This includes a **fair wage**, security, safe conditions, and access to healthcare. However, global demand for cheap clothing is a major reason why some garment factories have inadequate or dangerous working conditions. These might include:

- cramped and hot conditions due to too many workers and machines being squashed into the available space in order to maximize productivity
- old, unsafe machines and inadequate light, leading to accidents
- 12–18 hour working days, seven days a week
- limited toilet and drink breaks
- limited sick leave
- low wages, sometimes as little as a 10p per hour (see table on page 51).

CONTRAST THE PAST

The term "sweatshop" was first used in the early 20th century for crowded, poorly lit factories and workshops in the United Kingdom and the United States. The workers were often children and were paid miniscule wages for working long hours in poor conditions. Over time, unions emerged to defend the rights of workers, and conditions improved. In 2012, however, around 2 million people work in sweatshop conditions worldwide, mainly in less economically developed countries (LEDCs) making clothes for the US clothing market.

Case study: Shivshankar

Shivshankar was six years old when a man arrived in his village in India offering him a good education and work. Instead, he was kidnapped and held captive in an illegal garment factory in Delhi.

"I was doing embroidery work on garments. If I made even a slight mistake they would shout abusive words and beat me. I used to work from 9.00 a.m. until one in the morning. Then … I would sweep the floor and sleep on the spot at my work station."

"One day I asked the owner about taking a few hours rest because I was not keeping well. He refused, even though I was ill and very weak."

Child labour is illegal in India, yet factory owners bribe police to ignore the practice. Shivshankar was lucky because an organization working to stop child labour rescued him. They reunited him with his parents and helped provide him with a good education.

Fairer clothing

The ethical trade movement tries to protect workers' rights through the supply chain, from factory to shop. For a company to sell more ethically produced clothing, it may have to spend more, train factory owners to treat workers well, and supply manufacturing work only to those factories with adequate working conditions. However, many garments are made in factories that subcontract some manufacturing processes to other businesses which may not treat their workers so ethically. Some companies work with independent groups, such as Ethical Trading Initiative, whose inspectors can trace and monitor different subcontractors involved in making particular garments.

In this fair trade factory, employees have light, space, and ventilation. They work with safe machines on comfortable chairs. Their shifts are not too long and they can take breaks.

Inputs and outputs

The clothing industry in the United Kingdom employed over 180,000 people and generated products worth £9.5 billion in 2004. The diagram below shows the inputs and outputs involved in this including energy, raw materials, waste, and products.

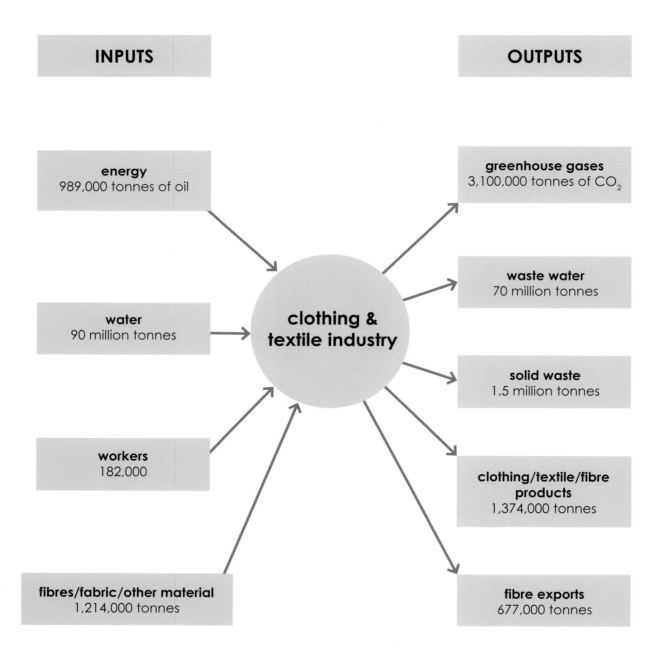

INPUTS

OUTPUTS

energy
989,000 tonnes of oil

water
90 million tonnes

workers
182,000

fibres/fabric/other material
1,214,000 tonnes

**clothing &
textile industry**

greenhouse gases
3,100,000 tonnes of CO_2

waste water
70 million tonnes

solid waste
1.5 million tonnes

**clothing/textile/fibre
products**
1,374,000 tonnes

fibre exports
677,000 tonnes

Reducing waste

Clothing factories produce a lot of waste. Fuel, water, and waste treatment costs are on the rise in the United Kingdom as in most countries. The industry as a whole needs to reduce both inputs and outputs in order to control cost.

A common practice is to order in more fabric than needed in case a certain design proves popular and more quantities of it need to be made as soon as possible. In addition, there are always lots of scraps of fabric left over after cutting. Some companies recycle these waste materials. Upcycling is when material is used to make different garments directly. For example, the brand From Somewhere uses waste jersey fabrics – originally destined to be used in other companies' garments – to create its own multi-coloured dresses. Factories can also reduce these waste materials by using technologies such as laser cutting to improve techniques.

> AROUND 15 PER CENT OF FABRIC INPUT INTO FASHION FACTORIES GOES TO WASTE.

Another important way to reduce waste and become more sustainable is to use less water. Levi's is using as little as 1.5 litres (2½ pints) of water per pair of jeans compared to 42 litres (74 pints) in the past.

WHAT HAVE WE LEARNED?

- Fashion factories are systems requiring input of materials, workers, and energy to output clothes.
- Production involves making patterns, cutting, sewing, and finishing. Many of these operations can be controlled by computer.
- Fashion factories are mostly in less developed countries to reduce costs. Many garment workers work in sweatshop conditions.
- Some clothing companies are trying to manufacture garments more sustainably and ethically to reduce the environmental and social impacts of their industry.

SELLING FASHION

As we have seen earlier, many designs will have been viewed and purchased by fashion buyers at a trade fair or fashion week. Once the clothing has been made, it needs to reach customers. This process involves transport from factory to shop, as well as producing marketing campaigns to entice customers to buy the garments.

Preparing to leave the factory

Finished garments are labelled, price-tagged, and packed. Each one is also given a unique identity using labels, barcodes or, increasingly, electronic tags. The items are scanned for entry on computer stock records or inventories. Inventories show exactly what a factory has made so that clothing companies know how many and which garments they can supply to shops. Companies may store finished, packed garments in warehouses or specialized distribution centres until they need to be sent on to stores. **Wholesalers** may store garments they have bought from different companies to supply outlets that stock many different brands, such as department stores.

These finished garments are being packed ready for distribution by road, rail, sea, and air.

Distribution

Logistics means controlling the efficient flow and storage of goods. This process can be manual, where workers select garments of the right size and colour off the shelves for packing and loading into vans. It can also be automated. For example, the Spanish company Zara has a giant, five-storey logistics centre in Spain, with over 200 kilometres (124 miles) of moving rails. Operators use computer programs that instruct only garments with particular electronic tags to move automatically along the rails to waiting trucks.

Vans and trains may generally deliver locally and nationally, and air freight and container ships internationally. The choice of transport depends on speed and cost. Delivery by plane can take just hours but is more expensive than an equivalent journey of days or weeks by sea.

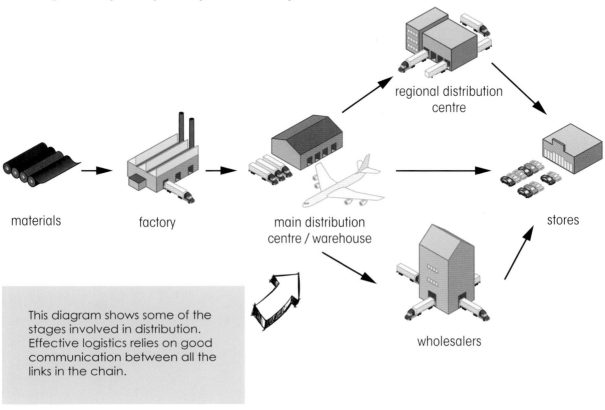

materials

factory

main distribution centre / warehouse

regional distribution centre

stores

wholesalers

This diagram shows some of the stages involved in distribution. Effective logistics relies on good communication between all the links in the chain.

ECO IMPACT

The following table compares four methods of transport by the carbon dioxide (CO_2) and nitrous oxides they release. Nitrous oxide gases contribute to acid rain as well as respiratory problems in people. The figures given are average number of grams of gas emitted per metric tonne of freight for each kilometre they are transported.

	aeroplane	lorry	train	ship
CO_2	500	60-150	30-100	10-40
nitrous oxides	5.56	1.85-5.65	0.2-1	0.26-0.58

Demand

Demand for hi-tech clothing, like any other product, is created by marketing. This is the business of promoting the attractive features of a product. Marketing includes advertising in the media, on billboards, and through television adverts. It also includes write-ups in fashion magazines that will focus on how hi-tech features add value to the garment.

Another way to create demand for a product is to get it endorsed by celebrities or to have it used on an expedition to an extreme environment such as Antarctica. An essential part of marketing is lifestyle branding, where people are informed how the clothing will fit into their life, or persuaded to aspire to a more glamorous life.

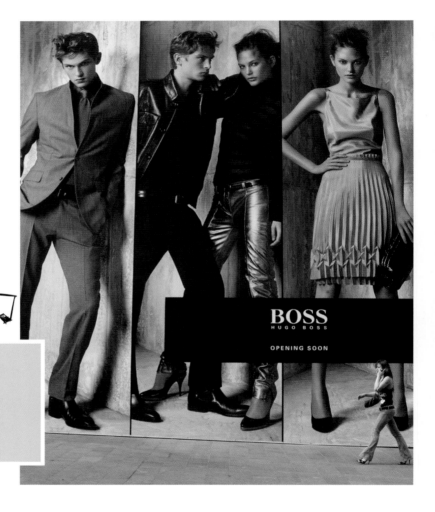

This giant billboard – spot the pedestrian in the right-hand corner! – is selling not only the clothes it displays but also a smart, urban, affluent lifestyle.

Shops have access to inventories of stock at the distribution centres and wholesalers supplying their clothes. When customers buy a product, the shops will update the stock inventories. This information about what items have been sold in different shops is used by companies to decide whether to send more or to manufacture more. This feedback from sales into the manufacturing system is important. It allows companies to supply what customers want and when.

Case study: Mass hi-tech

In 2011, the Japanese retailer Uniqlo had 1,000 shops globally but none in the United States. It started to get into the US market by establishing a foothold in the fashion capital New York. Uniqlo built two flagship stores in the city centre and put adverts on city buses and underground trains with messages such as "Uniqlo is beauty in hyper practicality". It created pop-up stores in areas of high traffic and at music festivals so more people would see the products. It used adverts featuring stars such as Charlize Theron and Orlando Bloom wearing Heattech clothing.

Heattech is a hi-tech fabric made using milk protein that retains body heat and **wicks** away sweat to keep the wearer dry. Around 100 million garments made of this fabric are sold each year. Other popular hi-tech Uniqlo products include light, packable down jackets.

Shin Odake, CEO of Uniqlo USA, has said: *"Following fashion trends is not what will make Uniqlo a household name … The US is the biggest economy in the world, the country is a big opportunity. We want to bring Heattech to Chicago … It's up to us to come up with new concepts and innovative merchandise so that the customer will want to spend."*

Marketing of hi-tech clothing needs to stress the features that make a company's products different and potentially life-improving. In this advert, Nike shows how these trainers can be connected to an iPod app that measures running performance.

GET BETTER, FASTER.
GET FREE.

NIKE FREE'S ENGINEERED FLEXIBILITY HELPS IGNITE THE MUSCLES IN YOUR BODY FROM THE GROUND UP FOR IMPROVED STRENGTH, BALANCE AND FLEXIBILITY — SO YOU GET EVEN MORE FROM YOUR WORKOUT. AND WHEN COMBINED WITH ONE OF THE 60 CUSTOM BUILT WORKOUTS FROM THE NEW NIKE TRAINING CLUB APP, YOU CAN REACH YOUR GOALS WHATEVER THEY ARE. EVER WANTED A PERSONAL TRAINER IN YOUR POCKET? NOW YOU'VE GOT ONE.

NIKE FREE
NIKE.COM/FREE

IN AND AFTER USE

Having been purchased and worn, the life cycle of an item of clothing continues until it is discarded, reused, or recycled. In the intervening period, a garment needs to be maintained, most obviously by washing and other cleaning processes. What impact does this have on the environment?

Fashion footprint

Every product has a carbon footprint. This is a measure of the carbon dioxide and other greenhouse gases released mostly through generation of electricity to run machines or to power vehicles for transport during a product's manufacture and use. Much of the footprint of any garment results from powering electrical **appliances** used for maintenance. Around 60 per cent of the total environmental impact of an average T-shirt can be greatly reduced by washing at cool temperatures, line rather than tumble drying, and not ironing. Consumers can cut down on maintenance not only by using appliances less, but also by using low energy-use appliances.

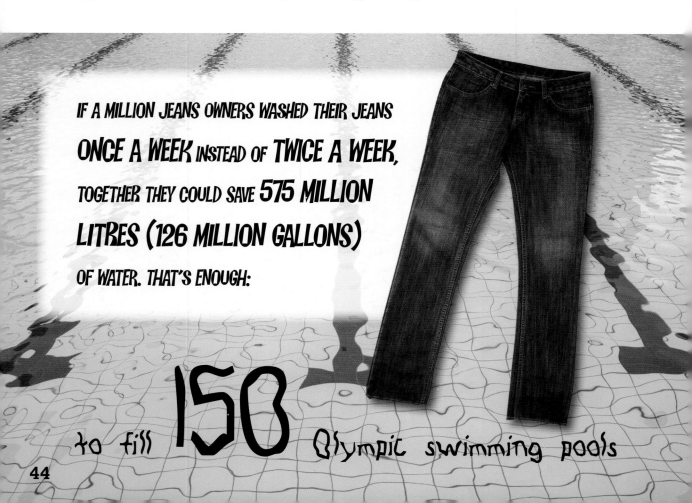

IF A MILLION JEANS OWNERS WASHED THEIR JEANS ONCE A WEEK INSTEAD OF TWICE A WEEK, TOGETHER THEY COULD SAVE 575 MILLION LITRES (126 MILLION GALLONS) OF WATER. THAT'S ENOUGH:

to fill 150 Olympic swimming pools

Reducing the number of times a garment is washed reduces the amount of freshwater used. A major problem with washing is the release into rivers of chemicals commonly found in detergents. These can encourage the growth of algae, which use up so much oxygen that fish and other organisms may die. Cleaning polluted water from factory processes can be expensive, and using lots of water in industry diverts it from other purposes, such as drinking or farming.

Some garments made of fine silks or hi-tech garments such as LED dresses, cannot be washed in water and need to be dry cleaned. Most dry cleaners use solvents that release harmful chemicals.

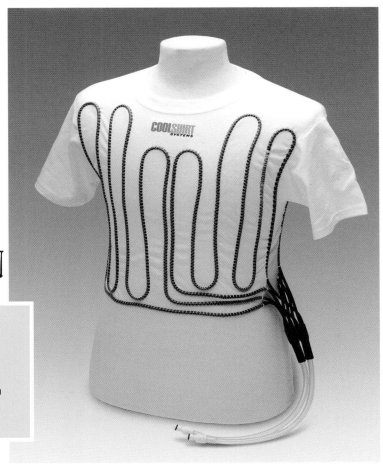

This Cool Shirt was designed to keep racing car drivers from overheating. It is maintained by refilling the pipes with cool liquid and recharging the pump which moves the liquid around.

Recycling and reuse

Owners of hi-tech garments may eventually not need them any more, however well they have maintained them. Sometimes parts such as electronics and zips will fail to work, holes will develop, and the garment may not be able to fulfil its function. Some manufacturers pledge to mend them where possible. For example, the US company North Face has a team of expert tailors and seamstresses who can replace zips and buttons, and patch fabrics. They have access to a store of spare parts in a wide range of colours and materials left over from making garments in previous years.

The secondhand trade

In 2010–2011, North Face donated 56,000 items it could not mend to Clothes4Souls, a US charity helping to donate to victims of natural disasters, patients in inner city hospitals, and many other people in the United States and globally. People give large quantities of clothing they have no further use for to clothes banks and to different charities, such as The Salvation Army or Oxfam. Charities give the clothes to the needy or sell them and use the money to fund a range of projects. Global trade in secondhand clothing is worth around US$1 billion (£627 million) a year. In some countries in Africa, such as Tanzania, secondhand clothes make up 30 per cent of import value, and people buy the majority of their clothes at thriving *mitumba* secondhand markets.

This secondhand stall is located at an outdoor market in Tunisia. Sources of cheap clothing like this are vital for poorer people around the world.

Case study: recycling

The US outdoor company Patagonia has a long history of using recycled materials, reducing the carbon footprint of its garments, and improving garment workers' rights. On top of this, it wanted to be more sustainable through the whole life cycle of its products. Patagonia partnered with eBay to make it easier for Patagonia product owners to sell unwanted items on to others. Another initiative was to run "buy less" marketing campaigns encouraging customers to avoid waste (but still buy their expensive, high-performing garments!).

Patagonia's other initiative has been to introduce "closed loop" recycling for their fleeces, which means turning worn out or damaged fleeces at the end of their life into new Patagonia garments. Owners return their fleeces to Patagonia who then transport them to the Japanese fibre manufacturer, Teijin. The fleeces are disintegrated into pellets and then these are chemically processed into fibres of the same quality as those made from crude oil, but using 20 per cent less energy and creating 80 per cent less CO_2. Fabrics made from these fibres are used in Patagonia factories to make fleeces and waterproofs.

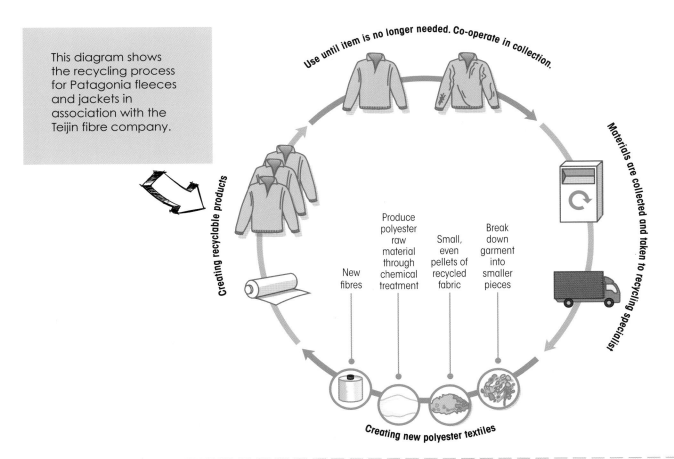

This diagram shows the recycling process for Patagonia fleeces and jackets in association with the Teijin fibre company.

Use until item is no longer needed. Co-operate in collection.

Materials are collected and taken to recycling specialist

Creating recyclable products

New fibres

Produce polyester raw material through chemical treatment

Small, even pellets of recycled fabric

Break down garment into smaller pieces

Creating new polyester textiles

Disposal

Most used clothing is not recycled. In the United Kingdom, 65 per cent of all clothing bought ends up in landfill sites, adding nearly 1.5 million tonnes of waste. Some clothing, along with other landfill waste, is burnt in incinerators that release energy that can be used to heat homes. Most, however, remains in landfill sites or dumps.

Many synthetic fabrics take decades to biodegrade (break down through the action of bacteria). On the plus side, this means the harmful products of biodegradation, including toxic gases, are released into the atmosphere very slowly. Natural fibres such as cotton and wool biodegrade quicker than synthetic fibres, but in the process they release methane gas, which contributes 23 times more to global warming than carbon dioxide. Hi-tech clothing including electronics can biodegrade in landfill, releasing poisonous metals that can leach or wash out into and pollute underground freshwater supplies. They require specialist disposal that separates out the different types of waste they contain.

In some countries, such as Egypt, some poor people spend their days sorting through hazardous rubbish in search of clothing. They can sell their finds to textile recyclers. Rag-pickers may rely on this work for their wages, but does this justify throwing away more clothes?

This jacket may look like it is made from leather but the fabric is, in fact, made in a laboratory using yeast, bacteria, and green tea! Using sustainable materials such as these may help reduce the environmental impact of the clothing industry in the future.

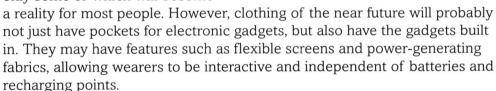

Fashion future

Hopefully, this book has given you some idea of the life cycle of hi-tech clothing. People are always coming up with new hi-tech fabrics, clothing inventions, and processing ideas, only some of which will become a reality for most people. However, clothing of the near future will probably not just have pockets for electronic gadgets, but also have the gadgets built in. They may have features such as flexible screens and power-generating fabrics, allowing wearers to be interactive and independent of batteries and recharging points.

Fashion in the future will increasingly be made of biodegradable synthetic fabrics that do not cause a landfill burden after use. Sustainability is a growing trend in clothing today that will only increase in the future. We could even see a shift from consumers buying cheaply made, throwaway fashion to more expensive but longer lasting, more adaptable clothes – for example, colour changing or temperature controlling garments. What manufacturers produce will always be strongly influenced by the buying choices we make.

WHAT HAVE WE LEARNED?
- Changes in clothing manufacture can help sustainability.
- Much of the environmental impact of a garment's life cycle happens when a consumer is using it.
- Individuals can take steps to reduce this impact.

TIMELINE

c. 5000 BC   Flax is used for wrapping Egyptian mummies. (Flax use dates back to pre-historic times.)

c. 3000 BC   Cotton is first used, and there is evidence of the spinning of wool.

c. 2600 BC   Silk is first used as a fabric in China.

1891   Count Hilaire de Chardonnet manufactures the first human-made fabric, artificial silk, out of natural cellulose from wood pulp or cotton rags.

1905   British silk firm Samuel Courtauld & Company produces viscose rayon.

1911   The American Viscose Corporation begins production of viscose rayon in the United States.

1938   Nylon is the first synthetic fibre to be made from oil and coal. It is strong, elastic, abrasion-resistant, and lustrous. They are first used for women's stockings, but then during World War II for parachutes and aeroplane tyres.

1941   Acrylic fibres are invented that have similar properties to wool. They are not used widely for clothing until the 1950s, when they appear under brand names such as Orlon.

1961   Aramid fibres are commercially produced and later used to make Kevlar. This is extremely strong, lightweight, flameproof, and wear resistant.

1962   Spandex is invented. This elastic synthetic fibre can stretch 500 per cent before breaking!

1972   The production of polyesters is greater than nylon for the first time.

1983   PBI (polybenzimidazole) fibres are created that do not melt, burn, or lose flexibility when exposed to flames. Used for firefighting suits.

FACTS AND FIGURES

The price of a running shoe

If a running shoe costs £100, how much of that money is used to pay factory workers and how much is spent on materials and other stages in its manufacture and sale? (The costs given below are typical figures.)

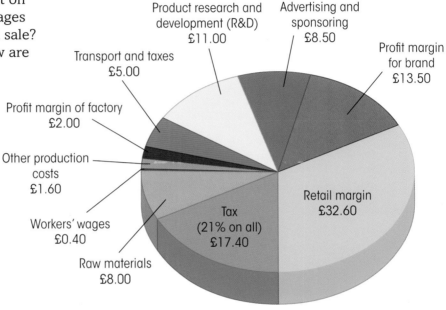

Product research and development (R&D)
£11.00

Advertising and sponsoring
£8.50

Profit margin for brand
£13.50

Transport and taxes
£5.00

Profit margin of factory
£2.00

Other production costs
£1.60

Workers' wages
£0.40

Raw materials
£8.00

Tax (21% on all)
£17.40

Retail margin
£32.60

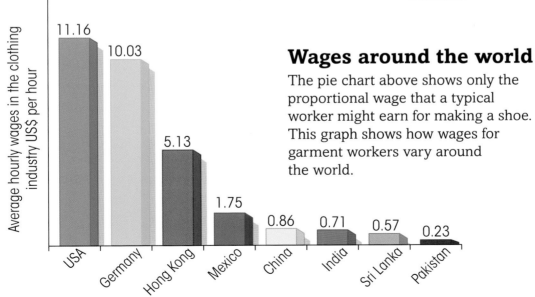

Wages around the world

The pie chart above shows only the proportional wage that a typical worker might earn for making a shoe. This graph shows how wages for garment workers vary around the world.

Average hourly wages in the clothing industry US$ per hour

USA — 11.16
Germany — 10.03
Hong Kong — 5.13
Mexico — 1.75
China — 0.86
India — 0.71
Sri Lanka — 0.57
Pakistan — 0.23

GLOSSARY

appliance machine, usually electrical, designed to perform a particular task

bespoke made to order

body scanner machine that measures and creates digital images of the body

brainstorming way of solving a problem by group discussion

branding creating a unique name and image for a product

component part of something bigger

constraint limitations on how something is made

conveyor belt loop of fabric or mesh rotating around two spaced wheels, used to transport objects

counterfeit make a copy of lesser value than the original, to sell deceptively as the original

criteria in design, standards or rules that dictate the features of a product

crude oil naturally occurring liquid oil used to make fuels and products including some textile fibres

digital tool device that enables someone to carry out a computer-based task

drag force acting against an object moving through water, air, or other medium

drape way fabric hangs, covers, or folds over an object

endorse give public support or approval for something

engineering design process of turning ideas into working products through stages of testing and selecting design solutions

ergonomics study of people's interaction with the objects in their working environment

fair wage wage that is enough to provide all the things a worker needs and is an accurate reflection of the work they do

fashion trend styles, colours, and other aspects of clothing that become popular

feedback process of using the output in a system to change the input. Feedback on which clothes people buy can be used to change the designs of clothing a company makes.

globalized connected to and interdependent with other people, businesses, or institutions worldwide

greenhouse gas gas, such as carbon dioxide, that contributes to the greenhouse effect. The greenhouse effect is the trapping of the Sun's warmth in Earth's atmosphere.

jersey fine, plain knit, slightly stretchy fabric made on machines from cotton, wool, or other fibres

logistics coordination of moving, storing, and supplying goods to people

lycra synthetic elastic fabric or fibre used to make closely fitted garments such as swimsuits

market researcher person who analyses sales and tastes in purchases to help companies make products that will be popular

microfibre fine synthetic fibre

migrant worker person who has moved to take a job, often because there is not enough work where they come from

modelling in design, creating an image of a planned object that accurately shows its form

nanotechnology engineering at a tiny scale, using atoms and molecules

natural fibre fibre that comes from plants and animals

optimization in design, improving, changing, or adapting designs to make them fulfil their function better

outsource when a company obtains goods or services from an outside supplier rather than make or do it themselves

patent authority from a government that allows a manufacturer sole right to make a product or component

prototype one of the first examples of a product to be made, so that it can be tested to make sure it works properly

public relations activities to maintain a favourable image for a company, product, or service

recycling processing old materials and products to make new materials and products. Recycling saves raw materials and reduces waste.

requirements in design, necessities affecting the cost or function of a final product or service

reverse engineer analyse and deconstruct something to see how it is put together in order to copy it

solvent substance in which another dissolves

specification list of requirements and constraints for a product

sustainability conserving an ecological balance by not using up natural resources and adopting methods that protect the environment

synthetic fibre fibre made from chemical resources such as oil and minerals

upcycling process of turning waste materials into new materials or products of better quality

VOCs Volatile Organic Compounds are materials that evaporate easily from sources such as vehicle exhausts and cleaning products. In sunlight, VOCs can react with atmospheric gases to create pollution.

wholesalers distributor who sells mainly to retailers and businesses, rather than consumers

wick absorb or draw away moisture

FIND OUT MORE

Books

Fashion Design Workshop: Stylish Step-by-Step Projects and Drawing Tips for Up-and-Coming Designers, Samantha Rei (Walter Foster Publishing, 2011)

Fashion Geek: Clothing, Accessories, Tech, Diana Eng (F&W, 2009)

Fashioning Technology: A DIY Intro to Smart Crafting, Syuzi Pakhchyan (Make, 2008)

My Fashion Lookbook, Jacky Bahbout (Thames & Hudson, 2012)

The Teen Vogue Handbook: An Insider's Guide to Careers in Fashion (Puffin, 2010)

Websites

antenna.sciencemuseum.org.uk/trashfashion/home/ wearwithoutwaste
This section of the Science Museum's website has a gallery of some interesting examples of environmentally friendly garments.

www.clearingthehurdles.org/index.html
Play Fair and other campaigning groups highlight poor working conditions at manufacturers for big sporting events. See how major sporting manufacturers did for the 2012 Olympics using the response chart on this website.

documentaryheaven.com/behind-the-swoosh
Could you survive the wages and conditions in a sweatshop? Watch this documentary about working conditions in a Nike factory in Indonesia.

www.ethicaltrade.org/in-action
Examine the work of the Ethical Trading Initiative, which is helping some companies improve conditions for their workers.

www.ilo.org/global/about-the-ilo/history/lang--en/index.htm
Interested in working conditions? Review the history of the International Labour Organization (ILO).

www.tomorrowsengineers.org
Visit this website to find out how to plan for a career in engineering.

Film

The Devil Wears Prada (20th Century Fox, 2006) starring Meryl Streep, Anne Hathaway, and Emily Blunt

Places to visit

Fashion and Textile Museum, London
www.ftmlondon.org
The Fashion and Textile Museum has exciting exhibitions on contemporary fashion, textiles, and jewellery.

Victoria and Albert Museum, London
www.vam.ac.uk
The V&A holds many fascinating collections of historical and contemporary fashion, as well as fashion drawings and illustrations to help you understand how designers have worked in the past.

Topics for further research

- Intrigued by the information about traceability on page 29? Then visit Patagonia's website and their Footprint Chronicles page. Here, you can select a garment and read about where it was designed, where materials were grown or produced, and where it was put together and distributed from. See the website: **www.patagonia.com/eu/enGB/footprint/index.jsp**

- Find out more about the ways manufacturers are making the life cycles of their garments more sustainable. Is there more they could do? How effective is the pressure consumers put on them? What are some ways we can influence them to adopt more environmentally friendly methods?

- Try to discover all you can about hi-tech fashion research and development. What are some trends that are currently occurring? Can you predict what sorts of hi-tech features our clothes might incorporate in 25 or 50 years time?

INDEX